<u>What Am I Looking At?</u>

50 elements
to help you make sense
of a work of art

By

Mariska Beekenkamp-Wladimiroff &

Juliana Beekenkamp

Introduction

There are many ways in which one can enjoy art. Often, many of us don't know where to start and feel a bit lost wandering through art collections, looking at things we don't really understand. Studying the history of art and the artistic process in which the work of art was produced can really help create a better understanding of what we are looking at.

However sometimes it is just the little things that make a huge difference; understanding little motifs within a work of art, the iconography, or symbolism of some of its elements, and even the use of particular colours.

In this booklet I have grouped together some (but by no means all!) of the motifs you might encounter when looking at art, in alphabetical order. It will hopefully help you in understanding some of the intended meaning. It can also shed a light on subconscious interpretations, or underlying feelings of artist and or viewer.

You can use these elements to hunt for representations in any works of art. Make it the theme of a trail in which you try to find a specific motif. Or you can look up elements you have noticed in a work of art to give you a deeper understanding.

In whatever way you wish to use this book, I hope that it will make looking at art more enjoyable and interesting!

Images discussed:

1. Almond/ Mandorla
2. Anchor
3. Apple
4. Arrow
5. Bare Breasts
6. (Small) Bird (Goldfinch)
7. Blue (the colour)
8. Book
9. Branch (laurel / olive)
10. Brown (the colour)
11. Candle
12. Circle / ball/ wheel / sun / Ouroboros
13. Clock, watch, time pieces, hour glass
14. Dog
15. Dove
16. Eagle
17. Fish
18. Flowers and Fruit in a Cornucopia (horn of plenty)
19. Garden
20. *Gold: See Orange*
21. Grapes (Vine)
22. Green (the colour)
23. Horns
24. Lamb
25. Lilly

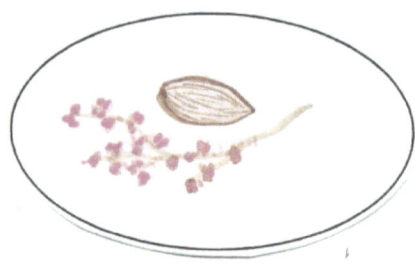

1. Almond / Mandorla *(2 circles overlapping creating an almond shape between them)*

- **Purity**
- **Promise** (because of its early blossom, and it's valuable content); **new life and fertility**
- **Watching out & protection**
- **Christian Figures:**
  - **Christ's majesty, glory and divinity**
  - **Virgin Mary**
  - Moses' elder brother **Aaron** carried a rod cut from an almond tree. It sprouted and therefore he was chosen leader of the 12 tribes of Israel.
  - **Joseph** was chosen as Mary's husband because his rod had miraculously started to bloom.
- **Assumption** (in Christian sense); **glory**

The almond shape is often surrounding Christian figures, it is an iconographic depiction of light.

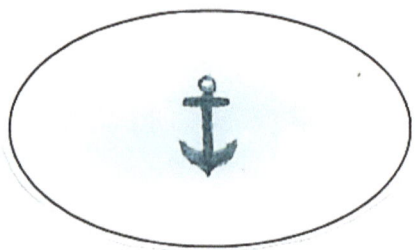

2. Anchor

- **Hope; safety; salvation**
- the anchoring influence of **Christ**
- In the first centuries A.D. it was sometimes used as an alternative to the cross, as an identifier of **Christianity**
- **St. Nicholas**, patron saint of seamen.

Of course, if you see an anchor on a grave or tattooed on someone's arm, it might just mean that they were / are sailors!

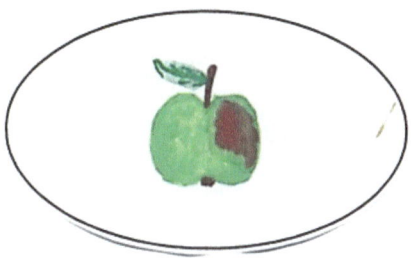

3. Apple:

- the forbidden fruit of the Garden of Eden; the fall of man / **sin**
- allusion to **Christ the redeemer**
- Mythology:
    - **Apple of Discord** (The Judgement of Paris)
    - **Aphrodite** (Greek) / **Venus** (Roman), goddess of **love**; other attributes: Dove (or other birds), scalloped shell

The Judgement of Paris:

In this Greek story three goddess's fight over a golden apple inscribed 'to the fairest!' and Paris of Troy is asked to choose the most beautiful woman.

The apple had been tossed into a wedding party by the Greek goddess of discord, Eris, because she had not been invited.

Hera, Athena and Aphrodite all fought over it, and tried to bribe Paris. Hera offered him power and Athena offered him wisdom. But it was Aphrodite who was chosen by Paris for she had promised him the love of his live: Helen of Sparta.

Helen, however, was already married. This became the cause of the Trojan War.

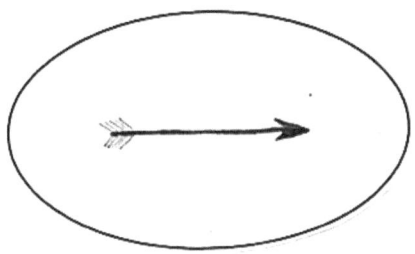

4. Arrow

- Attribute of **Cupid** (Roman) / **Eros** (Greek) (gold: love; lead: hate); lust
- Mythology:
    - **Apollo**, god of light, archery, peace and the arts; other attributes: laurel
    - **Diana** (Roman) / **Artemis** (Greek), goddess of childbirth and women, the hunt, and the moon; other attributes: elements to do with the hunt, half crescent moon
    - **Achilles,** Greek hero during the Trojan War, who died because of a poisonous arrow shot in his heel; other attributes: armour and weapons
- Saints & Martyrs:
    - **St Augustine, St Ursula, St Sebastian, St Christina, St Francis, St Dominic**
- Piercing a heart: **devotion**, union

- Personification of **America** (1 of the 4 parts of the world: Europe, Africa, Asia and America)
- Attribute of **concord** (agreement); here the arrows are often bundled as prove that they are no longer needed in the conflict.

It will be hard to find a Western historic art collection without at least one image of St Sebastian.
St Sebastian was the patron saint of archers, athletes and soldiers. He was believed to help in the protection against plagues. St Sebastian will be represented covered in arrows piercing his body.

The Golden Legend (1260) by Jacobus de Voragine became a late medieval bestseller, describing the lives of saints and ecclesiastical leaders. The book was often used when representing saints in the arts.

When looking at portrait paintings which include arrows, one can assume that depending on other elements like clothing or halos, we could either be looking at any of the figures above, or at a sitter who associates him or herself with any of these people.

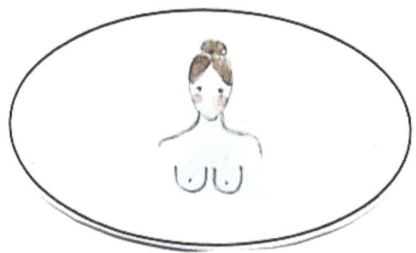

5. Bare breasts

- **Abundance and fertility** (Goddess of fertility, sometimes with many breasts)
- **Mother Nature**, often accompanied with other elements like flowers and fruits
- **Charity**; other elements often present: 3 children
- 1 of the 7 acts of mercy (Matthew 25:35-6): **tending the: thirsty**, hungry, stranger, naked, sick, the prisoner, burying the dead
- **Mercy**
- **Repentance**
- **Humility**

Sometimes breasts are depicted in peculiar ways, such as being presented on a plate. Breasts on a dish are the symbol of **St Agatha** - a gruesomely visible image of how she was martyred!

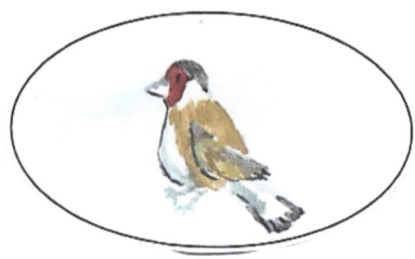

6. *small* Bird (Goldfinch)

- **the Passion** because of legends concerning Christ and small birds; Resurrection of Christ
- **Love**
- **The Soul**
- One of the 4 elements: **Air**, earth, water, fire
- **Allegory of Spring**

During the 17th century small birds were often kept as pets by young children. Christ might be holding a small bird to make him look like any human child.

There are several stories relating to Christ and small birds. He is described as having made clay birds come to life, and on the road to Calvary a small bird picked one of the thorns from Christ's crown out of his forehead which created a bloodstain on the bird.

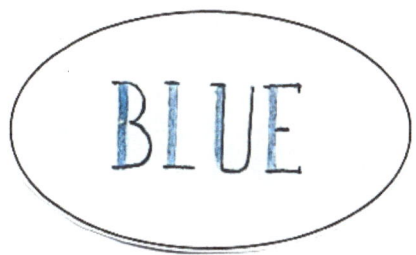

7. Blue (the colour)

- The Virgin **Mary**
- **Purity**, truth and clarity
- **Heaven**; infinity
- Search for **redemption**; despair

Before synthetic colours, a bright colour blue was hard to obtain. Artists would use Lapis Lazuli stones, which had to make the long journey from what is now Southern Afghanistan, grind them down and mix them with chemicals to get rid of any impurities. The result was a beautiful bright and strong blue, but also an extremely expensive colour! This became even worse when the church put a strict control on the colour in the 13th century. As a result this colour was often restricted to Mary's cloak and small elements within the painting.

Blue seems to be the colour of the unattainable. It is expensive to produce, and it is a colour we associate with distance.

This might have to do with the inability of our eyes to see most colours in the far away distance, except for blue. Artists make use of this in what is called **Atmospheric Perspective**, or **Aerial Perspective**. They use the colour blue to create depth in a painting, since our brain will automatically register this colour as something which must be far away.

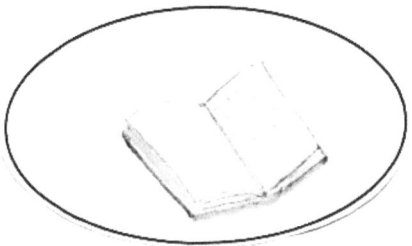

8. Book

- **Wisdom; enduring knowledge**
- **Reason**
- Christianity:
    - Attribute of the **Virgin Mary** (for other attributes, see: the Virgin Mary)
    - Attribute of the **Apostle Paul** (other attribute: sword)
    - Attribute of **St Jerome**, who is credited with translating the bible into Latin: *The Vulgate* (other attributes: lion, church, red cloak)

Books used to be handmade, precious objects, often made by monks. Even after the invention of the printing press (1450), books remained objects of human effort, wisdom and history. This is possibly why over the centuries people have turned to burning books, in an effort to send a strong symbolic message.

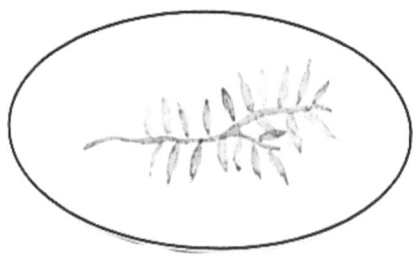

9. Branch (laurel / olive)

Laurel:

- Mythology: **Apollo & Daphne**: Apollo god of the arts and the sun fell in love with Daphne, who did not return his love. While being chased by Apollo her father, hearing her cries, turned her into a laurel tree. Daphne was a great athlete and very fast runner, which is why winners of competitions often get crowned with laurel leaves: **victory, triumph**
- **Immortality** (victory over death)
- **Honour; Fame**
- Reference to the person being **artistic** or literary; 1 of the 7 Liberal Arts (Grammar, Rhetoric, Logic, Mathematics, Geometry, Music, Astronomy): **Logic**, carries a laurel bush (other attributes: Snake symbol of Prudence and argument, flowers, scales)

Olive:

- **Peace;** Concord, **agreement;** harmony
- **Immortality,** renewal
- **Healing**
- **Last moments of Christ in Garden of Gethsemane** at of the Mount of Olives, Jerusalem, before he is arrested.
- In Mythology: symbol of:
  - **Pallas Athena** (Greek) / **Minerva** (Roman): goddess of **wisdom** and **the arts**, war to defend all things good, not to destruct

It is the tree which is rooted in the earth but its branches reach out to the heavens, this is probably why branches are often used as symbols.

People in power often hold rods or staffs. The personification of Grammar (1 of the 7 Liberal Arts; other attributes; children, parchment) holds a rod to punish children's mistakes!

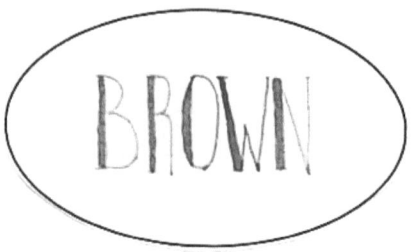

10. Brown (the colour)

- The **earth, humanity**
- **Poverty and humility** (hence the colour of cloaks of monks)
- **Simplicity**
- **Dependability**

In the beginning of the 19th century, scientists began to ask questions about colour: How does our brain interpret colours? Which colours contrast each other? Which colours are seen as attractive together? They confirmed what many artists had long known, but it generated a whole new interest in the power of colours.

Brown is often used as the ground colour on a canvas painting.

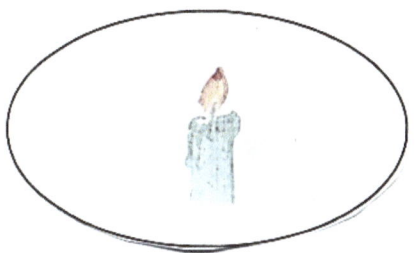

11. Candle

- **Faith**
- **The eye of God**
- **Charity**
- Extinguished candles: **memento mori**, or reminders of death; fleetingness of human life
- Christianity:
  - **Christ**: light of the world
  - **St Bridget** would use dripping candle wax to simulate Christ's wounds
  - **St Genevieve**: on two occasions God miraculously relit candles that she was holding.
  - **St Lucia/Lucy** (meaning light) is associated with the festival of light, because her feast day falls on the Winter Solstice, the shortest day of the year. Other symbols: eyes, lamp, dagger.

Especially in Scandinavian countries the festival of St Lucia is celebrated with girls wearing crowns with burning candles.

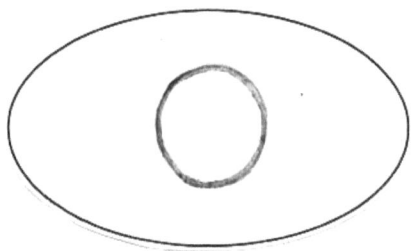

12. Circle / Ball / Wheel / Sun / Ouroboros

- The spiritual and eternal world, representation of **heaven;** perfect, endless, infinite, divine
- **Ouroboros**: snake biting its own tail; symbol of **eternity**
- Seen as the perfect shape during the Renaissance- conforming to the concept of **God**, and seen as the ultimate **artistic skill**: drawing a perfect circle in a single motion
- **Unity**, infinity, democracy and an assembly of equal
- **Creation**; the **Sun**; mother earth; the feminine spirit; God; the circle of life
- **Sovereign's Orb:** symbolising dominion
- **Wheel: time and faith; fortune**

- In mythology:
  - symbol of **Zeus** (Greek) **/Jupiter** (Roman) as sky god
  - representing the wheels of the chariot of **Helios** (Greek) **/Apollo** (Roman)

- In Christianity:
  - symbol of **St Catherine**, who was martyred on a wheel
  - **St Nicolas**, patron of sailors and children (a Father Christmas figure even now in some cultures) - the 3 golden balls are a reference to his help of a father who had no money for the dowry of his 3 daughters.

N.B: With shapes look out for how artists group elements within the painting or align things - there might not be an actual physical shape present!

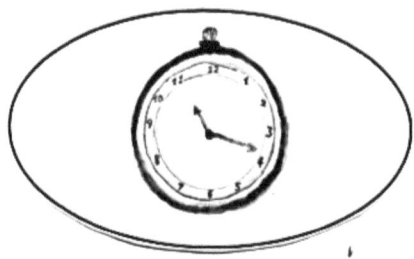

13. Clock/ watch/ time pieces/ hour glass

- For a long time they were seen as objects of wonder + economic prosperity (**materialism**)
- Part of the 5 senses: **hearing**
- Metaphor for **God**, the universe, and the solar system; representing a rational, natural and orderly world
- **Destiny**
- **Temperance, reason**
- Reference to the passing of time, the **brevity of existence; death**
- **Vanity & transience:** when our time has come, we will be judged for eternal redemption
- **Rhythm of life**
- **Artist's ability** and **skill**: to outlive the things he paints, to stop time and preserve the things he paints, but also the difficulty of investing a work of art with time

How to tell a whole story is one of the hardest things if you only have one two-dimensional canvas. This was largely the reason why traditionally artists who were able to depict stories in art (history paintings: depicting mythological, biblical, and later contemporary historical events) were seen as the most capable and skilled. Instilling a canvas with a sense of movement in time is one of the greatest things an artist could achieve.

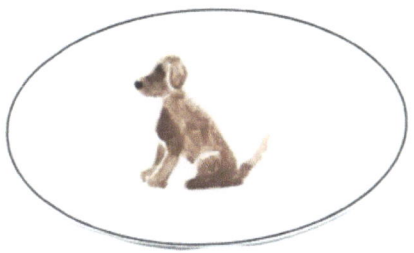

14. Dog

- **Faithfulness, fidelity, loyalty,** watchfulness
- **Lust, shamelessness, guards of Satan**

Like so many subjects, dogs can be either positive or negative. All depends on other elements within the work of art, and you will have to hunt for other clues to decipher the meaning.

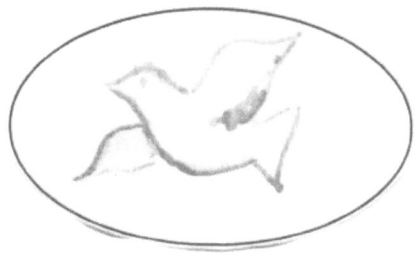

15. Dove

- Christianity:
  - o **Holy Spirit**
  - o **Annunciation**
  - o **Baptism**
- **Innocence; purity**
- **Love; peace,** often accompanied with an olive branch
- **The soul**
- Mythology:
  - o **Venus /Aphrodite**, goddess of love
  - o **Athena,** goddess of peace

There are many references to doves in the Bible, and it is one of the most enduring sentimental symbols.

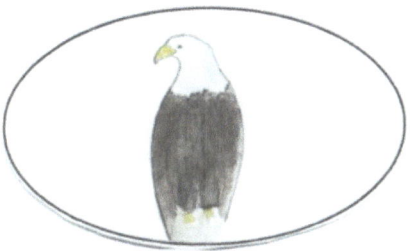

16. Eagle

- Symbol of all **celestial powers**
- **Royalty; authority; strength**
- **Victory**
- Mythology: **Jupiter**: god of the sky and thunder, the eagle holds Jupiter's thunder bolts
- Christianity: 1 of the 4 **beasts of the Apocalypse**

The eagle is a popular national symbol for many countries, present in military insignia and heraldry.

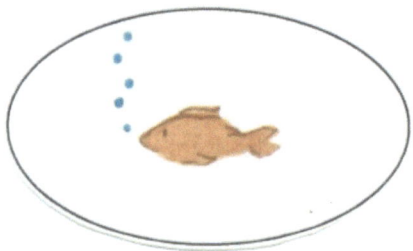

17. Fish

- Christianity:
  - **Jesus Christ** (In Greek, "Iesous Christos Theou Yios Soter" means "Jesus Christ, Son of God the Saviour", the initial letters of five Greek words form the word for fish *Ichthys*)
  - **Baptism**
  - **Raphael leading Tobias** to use the miraculous fish whose heart, liver and gall were to restore his father's sight, and drive the demons from his bride.
- **Fertility and creation, the womb; re-birth**
- Mythology:
  - **Salacia**: wife of Neptune, goddess of the sea.
  - **Venus / Aphrodite**: goddess love. She was worshipped by her followers on her sacred day, Friday, when fish would be eaten.

Fish are often mentioned in the Bible, and feature in many stories. This is of course not surprising as fish was a staple diet in this part of the world. The Apostles were also often referred to as 'fishers of men'.

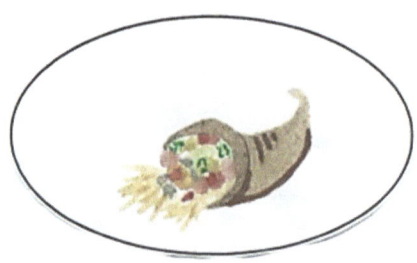

18. Flowers and Fruit (Cornucopia *or horn of plenty*)

- **Fertility; abundance; fortune; Autumn**
- Mythology:
  - Goddess **Ceres**: agriculture and fertility
  - **Jupiter** (Roman) / **Zeus** (Greek) gave a goat's horn to his nursemaid as a thank you, and the horn would fill with anything she wished for. (cornucopia)
  - **Fortuna** (Roman) **/ Tyche** (Greek): goddesses of good fortune and luck. Other attributes: ball, wheel.
  - **Concordia (Homonoia):** goddess of agreement, understanding, national and marital harmony; other attributes: patera (sacrificial bowl), caduceus staff (symbol of peace).
  - **Lares:** Roman guardian deities
  - **Flora:** Roman goddess of flowers and the season of spring

- One of the 4 elements: **'Earth'**, 'Water', 'Air' and 'Fire'.
- 1 of the 7 Liberal Arts (Grammar, Rhetoric, Logic, Mathematics, Geometry, Music, Astronomy): **Logic**, sometimes holds flowers (other attributes: Snake symbol of Prudence and argument, laurel bush, scales)
- **Peace; Concord**
- **Europe**

Leaders often use the cornucopia to symbolize all the good things that their leadership bring, and so it is a favourite in images of peace and good governance.

Note that different types of fruit and or flowers can mean different things, and some are mentioned in this book.

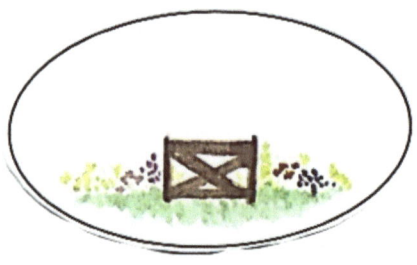

19. Garden

- **Paradise**
- Enclosed gardens represent the **Virgin Mary**

Imaginary gardens with beautiful young couples and plenty of symbols that refer to love and marital fidelity were a very popular theme especially in 17th century Holland, and 18th century France. They were often referred to as 'Fête Champêtre'.

20. *Gold: see Orange*

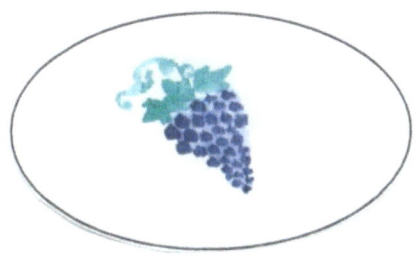

21. Grapes

- **Wisdom**
- Mythology: **Bacchus** (Roman) / **Dionysos** (Greek), god of wine and festivities (Often accompanied by satyrs (lust) and maenads (nymphs))
- **Sacrifice** (as wine resembles the colour of blood); the **Eucharist**
- **Autumn**

Vine

- **Love and friendship**
- **Faithfulness**
- **Christ**

Grapes and vines are usually references to fertility and prosperity, and this has been the case throughout history.

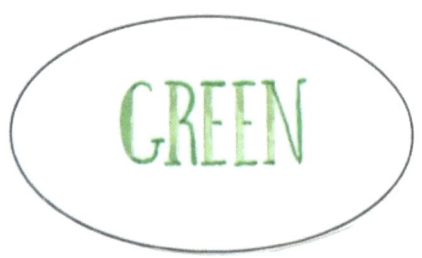

22. Green (the colour)

Positive meanings:

- **Calm**
- **Nature & environmentalism**
- **Life & youthfulness; Fertility; Season of Spring**
- **Hope & optimism; Peace**
- **The Holy Spirit** (In Christian Orthodox churches)

Negative meanings:

- **Envy**
- **Death**
- **Temptation**
- **Inexperienced**
- **Sick**

Before the 19th century artists found it very difficult to get the right colour green. Pigments were limited and colours often changed over time, leaving us with some funny looking paintings! Have a look at the vegetation on some pre 19th century paintings, anything seem wrong? Possibly bright blue vegetation? This is most likely the result of the yellow fainting away!

It was only in 1814 when a copper and arsenic containing green was invented, called 'Vert Veronese'.

According to Kadinsky green implies utter complacence and absolute rest - boring but reassuring!

The calming effects of green might be the reason why many schools use it.

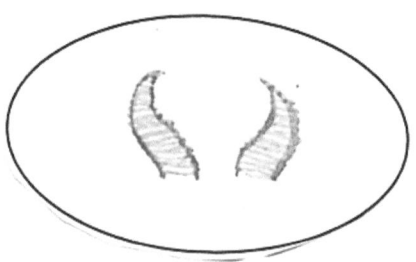

23. Horns

- **Moses**: because of multiple possible translations of the Latin word: *'cornutam'* (horn/shine/flashing with rays of light), Moses sometimes is depicted with horns!
- **Strength; victory**
- Mythology:
    - A keros: cup in the form of a horn, often held by **Dionysus**: god of wine
    - **Horn of plenty**: see also cornucopia: **Jupiter** (Roman / Zeus (Greek)gave a goat's horn to his nursemaid as a thank you, the horn would fill with anything she wished for. Also symbol of **Fortuna** (Roman) / **Tyche** (Greek).
    - **Pan:** Greek god of nature, personification of lust.
- **Phallic symbol**; male fertility
- The **crescent moon; the night; the devil** (usually in this case the horns point outwards or down)

Horns are seen as symbols of strength, the weapon with which the animals fight, and therefore the trophy for those that kill them.

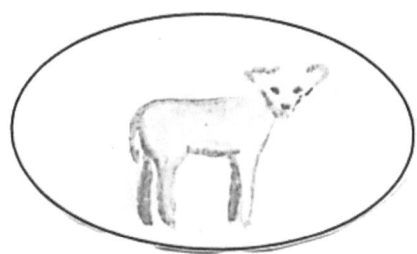

24. Lamb

- Christianity:
    - **Jesus**, the lamb of God (Agnus Dei)
    - **Sacrificial offering** and Christ's sacrificial death to save humanity
    - With a banner: the risen **Christ triumphant over death**.
    - With a cross and a gash in its side: **the passion of Christ**.
    - Seated on a throne or a book: **the judgment of Christ**.
    - In John 1:29 John the Baptist says: "Behold the Lamb of God who takes away the sin of the world" when he sees Jesus. **John the Baptist** is often accompanied by a lamb. Other attributes: dressed in camel skin, reed cross, with a bowl or shell for scooping up the water to baptize, river.

- **Renewal**
- **Innocence**

In many cultures lambs were sacrificed to assure salvation.

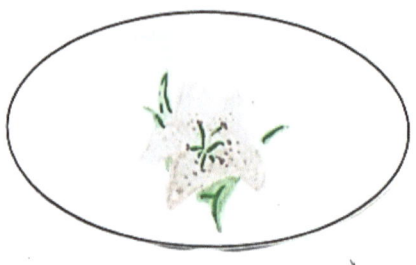

25. Lily

- **Purity (white); virginity; Annunciation**
- **Fertility**
- **Peace**
- **Christianity:**
    - **Virgin Mary; divinity**
    - **Susanna (meaning lily):** a married woman, is spied upon by 2 old judges while bathing in her garden. They attempt to force themselves upon her, saying that if she does not submit, they will accuse her of adultery. With Daniel's assistance, Susanna's innocence is established, and the two elders are put to death. **Symbol of the saved soul, and marital chastity**
- Mythology: **Juno** (Roman) / **Hera** (Greek): chief goddess of Olympus, protector of women, childbirth and marriage. It was believed that the lily was created from her milk.

A "fleur-de-lis" is a stylized symbol of the lily, often used in heraldry, and is especially associated with France and its monarchy.

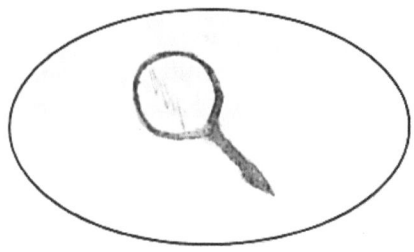

26. Mirror

- **Illusion, deception**
- **Wisdom and self-knowledge; Prudence (sensible) and Truth**
- 1 of the 7 deadly sins: anger, greed, laziness, **pride (vanity)**, lust, envy, and extravagance.
- 1 of the 5 senses: Hearing, feeling, **sight**, smell, taste
- Mythology:
  - **Narcissus:** the beautiful boy who falls in love with his own reflection so much that one morning, he fell into the lake and drowned.
  - **Venus / Aphrodite**
- **Purity; Virgin Mary**

Artists can use a mirror in their painting to show us something we would otherwise not see. This can create depth, an extra layer of meaning, or an intriguing story line.

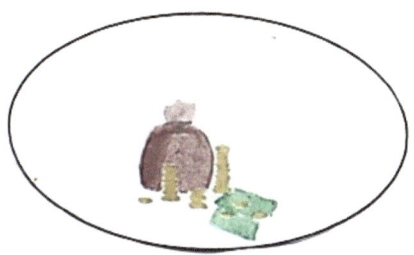

27. Money

- Tax gatherer; calling of **St Matthew**
- **Tribute money**
- **Judas**
- **Greed**
- **Vanitas**
- Mythology**:**
  - **Danea**: seduced by the god Zeus who came down to earth from Mount Olympus in a shower of gold; symbol of the corrupting effect of wealth
  - **Hermes**: god of gain and riches; symbol of commerce; other attributes:
- **Lais of Corinth**: courtesan of ancient Greece
- **Charity**: when shaken out of a purse

Art can have a somewhat uneasy relationship with money. Creativity, we now believe, should not be dictated by money. However, even the greatest artists like Leonardo da Vinci, were restricted by how much money they could spend on materials, or subject matters they were allowed to depict!

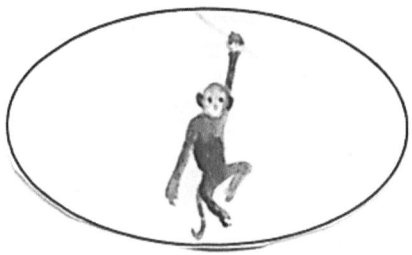

28. Monkey

- **Greed and over-indulgence**
- **Lust**
- **Shamelessness**
- The **devil**, and vice in general
- **Parody of man**
- **Skill of imitation: arts and artists**

Monkeys are often funny and uncannily like we are, this is why we enjoy seeing them in familiar human situations, something that artists have used in many works of art.

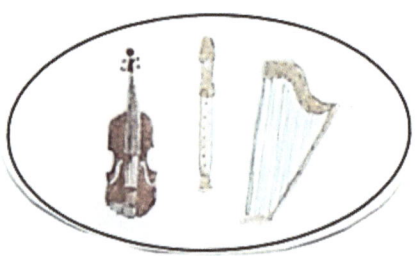

29. Musical Instruments

- **love and seduction**
- **brevity and transitory nature of life; heaven**
- **harmony**
- 1 of the 5 senses: **hearing**
- Mythology:
    - **Orpheus**: Orpheus had the power to enchant with his music not only all living creatures, but also the trees and the rocks
- Christianity: **King David**, 2nd king of Israel, author of Psalms

This is another element which meaning is dependent on other elements within the work of art. The fact that music brings people together with different personalities – like different notes – blending together to create something beautiful, also creates a tension - especially when it concerns young men and women!

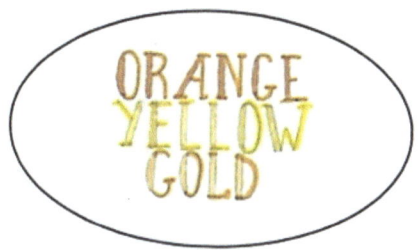

30. Orange (the colour)

- **Indulgence**
- **Carnal desires, original sin**
- **Corruption, Judas** the betrayer of Christ

N.B: Sometimes it is hard to make out if something is orange, yellow or gold. Unlike the colour orange, yellow and gold have more positive connotations, and so you might have to look for other clues.

50. Yellow

- **Miracles,**
- **Harmony**
- **Sustenance of the soul**
- **Renewal, hope, light and purity**

20. Gold

- **Majesty**
- **The Sun**
- **Sacredness**

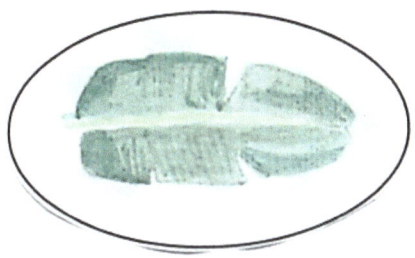

31. Palm Leaf

- **Military victory**
- Christian's **victory over death**
- **Martyrdom**
- **Fame**
- **Chastity**
- **Asia** personified
- **Abundance and plenty**

Palm leaves are not always easy to distinguish. The ways artists used to depict them often looks more like a giant green feather! Once you have spotted one though, it will be very easy to find plenty more in most historical collections.

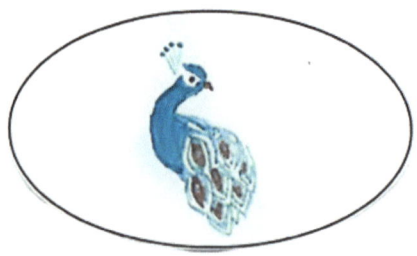

32. Peacock

- **Resurrection; immortality** (Ancient myths said that the flesh of a peafowl did not decay after death)
- **Love**
- Mythology: **Juno** (Roman) **/ Hera** (Greek), goddess of women, marriage and childbirth
- Dangerous **pride**

Peacocks have been a favourite ornamental motif for millennia and across many different cultures. Especially near the end of the 19th century peacock motifs became extremely popular in Western art.

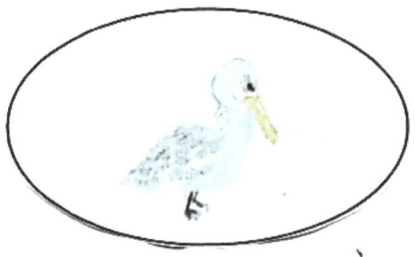

33. Pelican

- **Christ's sacrifice**
- **Death; the afterlife**

A pelican was believed to feed its young with its own blood. This myth was the basis of many depictions in Christian churches, but also its use in heraldry.

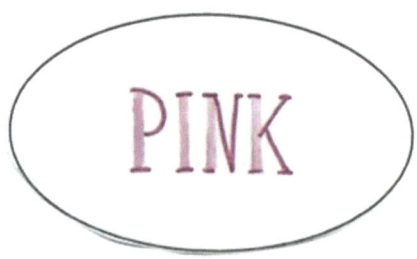

34. Pink (the colour)

- **Eternal innocence**
- **The Virgin Mary; Virgin and Child; The Immaculate Conception**
- **Nurture, love, harmony**
- **Kindness, compassion**

Until the beginning of the 20th century pink was considered a colour for boys, and blue for girls! (Possibly to do with blue being associated with the Virgin Mary, or it being a more passive colour).

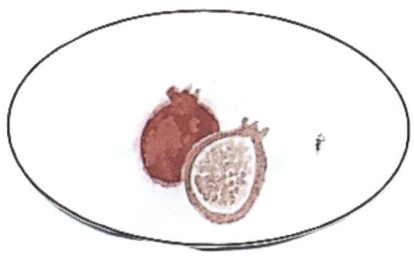

35. Pomegranate

- **Immortality; eternal life; resurrection**
- **Spring; fertility; prosperity**
- The **Christian church** and all its members
- Symbol of **the Passion**: its red coloured juices referring to Christ's blood
- Greek myth of **Persephone**, who could only return from the underworld 6 months out of the year, beginning in Spring, because she had eaten the seeds of the pomegranate.

The pomegranate tree has an ancient origin, and in many cultures it is supposed to bring good fortune and riches.

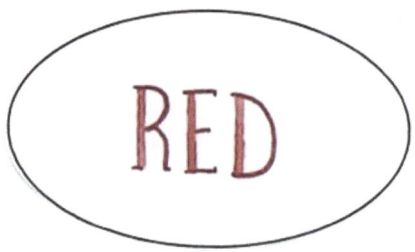

36. Red (the colour)

- **Greediness, power and lust**
- **Martyrdom; redemption**
- **Blood, symbol of life**
- **Family lineage and love**

Try to imagine what the work of art would look like if you changed the colour red for another colour... It will most likely give it a completely different feel, and change how you interpret the work of art.

Red is a warm colour and usually tends to liven an image up.

Any red fruits are often a symbol of the Passion (the last events in Christ's life), with the red coloured juices referring to Christ's blood.

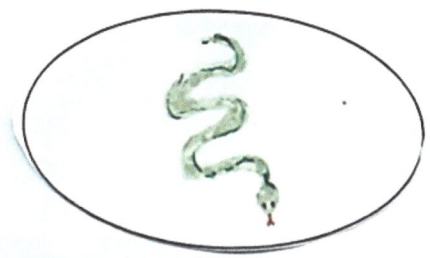

37. Serpent / snake

- **Rejuvenation**
- **Wisdom**, **Prudence** and reasoned judgment;
  Logic: 1 of the 7 Liberal Arts (other attributes:
  laurel bush or flowers, scales)
- **Guardians**
- Mythology:
  - **Asclepius** /Apollo god of medicine and
    healing, attributed with a serpent
    curling around a rod.
  - Caduceus: **Hermes** (Roman)/ **Mercury**
    (Greek) staff: *two* snakes curling around
    a rod; Hermes / Mercury is the guide of
    the gods
  - **Medusa**: a monster, with a female face
    and snakes in place of hair. Gazing
    directly upon her would supposedly
    turn onlookers to stone!
- **Moses:** story of the serpent on a pole which
  Moses erected so that anyone looking at it
  would be cured

- But also **Satan** and original **sin; deceit**

It is unclear what creature tempted Eve to eat the fruit from the tree of knowledge. However, since it was made to crawl on its belly after being cursed by God, it takes the shape of a snake in many images. In the 13th century the serpent sometimes has a woman's face.

Snakes; symbols of rejuvenation (since the snake changes its skin) and their poison which like a drug can harm or help depending on the quantity, are still used today on ambulances and in logos associated with doctors and medicine.

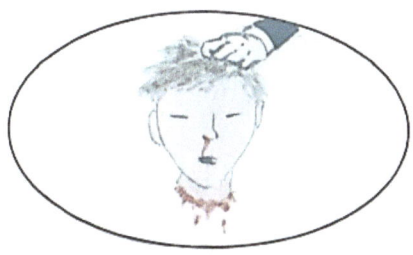

38. Severed head

- Christianity:
  - Story of **David and Goliath**: shepherd boy David comes to the rescue of the Israelites by killing the giant Goliath and securing his people's victory.
  - **John the Baptist** and **Salome**, the femme fatale: Salome's mother wanted revenge on St John the Baptist after he had condemned her from marrying again, she let Salome "seduce" her stepfather Herod with a dance, asking him for the head of John the Baptist on a platter.
  - **Judith**: Jewish patriotic heroin who saved the besieged city of Bethulia of the Assyrian army, by enamouring their commander Holofernes, and beheading him.
  - **Saint Dennis,** who is said to have gone to Paris carrying with him his severed head.

- **Life disjointed from feelings**
- Allegory of man's misfortunes at the hands of a scheming woman (like Salome); **productive & destructive forces of female sexuality**
- Patrician Carrying heads (although not of the bloody type!): **lineage**. Reflects a patriarchal Roman custom of making a wax image of the head of the family when he died, keeping it in the family shrine/altar, and carrying it in funeral processions!

The head is often considered the seat of the soul and the source of a person's strength, giving it extraordinary sacral value.

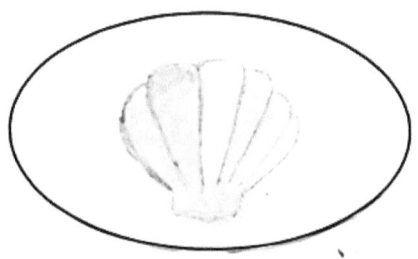

39. Shells /oysters/ mussels

- **Fertility; birth**
- **Love; sexual passion** (the two halves either opened or closed...!)
- Mythology: **Venus** (Roman) / Aphrodite (Greek) who was born of the sea
- **Virgin Mary**
- **Pilgrimage**
- **Baptism**

Sea shells are little gifts from the sea, sometimes edible, often pretty and if you are very lucky it might hold a surprise inside! No wonder it has such positive meaning. During the 18th century it inspired a whole art movement and style called the **Rococo**.

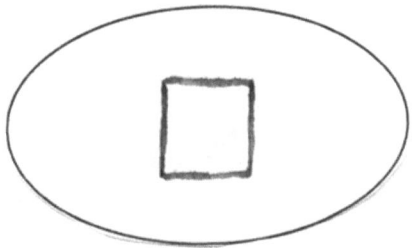

40. Square

- the solid physical world, **the earth,** kingship
- **4 corners of the world, 4 continents, 4 cardinal points** (north, east, south, west), **4 seasons,** division of the day (dawn, day, evening, and night), **4 elements** (fire, water, earth and air) – with Christ/God in the middle
- Square halos were sometimes used for **the living**

Straight lines and straight corners are not something you will see in nature, and a real sign of civilization. It is therefore very fitting the see the square as a representation of material, man made things.

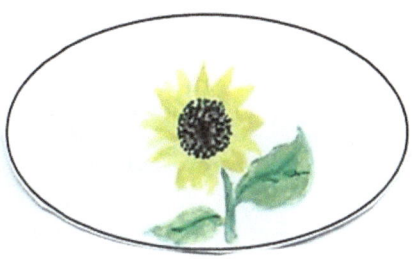

41. Sunflowers

- Mythology: **Clytie**, who turns into a sunflower, after the sun god Apollo does not return her love.
- **Devotion; loyalty** to god and king.
- The **sun**
- Because they follow the sun, sunflowers are seen as a **connection between the earth and heaven;** linked with theories that for every plant there exists a correlated star – and for the sunflower this is the sun.
- Once dead, the seeds bare the **potential for life; longevity**
- **Hope**
- **The human soul**

Aestheticism was an art movement from 1870 to 1900. One of its favourite motifs was the sunflower, as they favoured strong and simple colours.

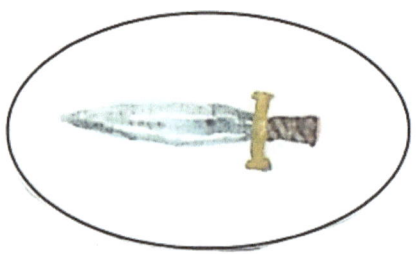

42. Sword

- **Authority**
- Administration of **Justice**; other attributes: scale
- **Fortitude**
- **Constancy**; other attributes: a pillar
- **Despair** (used to kill herself)
- Symbol of **Vanitas**
- One of the 7 liberal arts: **Rhetoric**
- One of the 4 temperaments: **Anger**
- **Melpomene**: muse of tragedy
- Christianity:
  - **Martyr**
  - The **Apostle Paul**; other attributes: book

A sword can be destructive, but also protective, so its power lies within the person who carries it.

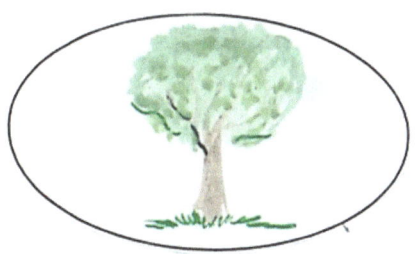

43. Tree

- **Tree of life, tree of knowledge**
- **Shelter; nourishment**
- **Virgin Mary**

In many cultures trees are sacred, and an important part of worship.

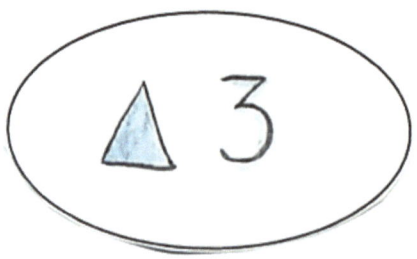

44. Triangle / Number 3

- Symbol of the **Holy Trinity** (God the Father, God the Son, and God the Holy Spirit)
- **Creation**
- A triangular halo belongs to **God**
- The all-seeing eye of God
- **Balance & harmony**
- Represents the **number 3**: triad of family - male, female, and child; beginning, middle and end; birth, life and death; the interdependence of all existence
- **Mother with 3 children: Charity**; Other attributes: A pelican (feeding its young with its own blood), Cornucopia, fruit (abundance; fortune), Dressed in red (love)
- **Face looking in 3 directions: Prudence** or wise conduct; past, present, future
- **Triple headed beast: Prudence**

The number three is important in many religions and folk tales and often has mystical and spiritual connotations. Not always is the number three represented in a triangle, but a triangle does represent the number three!

Even if the triangle is not obviously visible, look out for the way in which for instance God the Father, God the Son, and The Holy Spirit are aligned. More often than not they will form a triangle between them.

Sometimes there are actual triangles present. For instance, on an icon in the National Gallery in London, which is ornamented on the outside with triangles and circles.

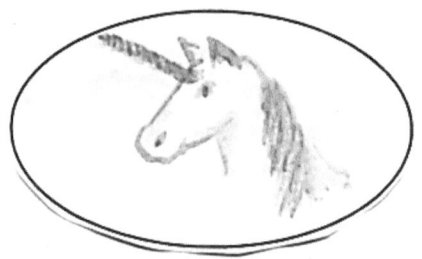

45. Unicorn

- **Virgin Mary**
- **Chastity; purity; virginity**

According to legend only a virgin maiden can catch and tame a unicorn.

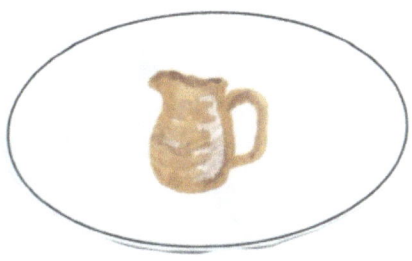

46. Urn / pitcher / vase

- Mythology:
    - **Neptune** (Roman) / **Poseidon** (Greek): god who rules the sea and its inhabitants
    - **Juventas** (Roman) / **Hebe** (Greek): goddess of youth, cupbearer for the gods and goddesses of Mount Olympus, serving their nectar and ambrosia, and making baths for Ares
- 1 of the 4 elements: fire, earth, air, and **water**; **allegory of a river**
- **A Spring**, perpetual renewal of nature
- Christianity:
    - **Wedding feast at Cana**: Christ's first miracle was turning water into wine at this wedding
    - 1 of 7 acts of Mercy: **Giving water to the thirsty**
    - **Baptism**

- **Purity & temperance** (for diluting: moderation, and to put out the fire of lust!)
- **Winter**

When a young girl is depicted with a broken urn or pitcher, this often indicates lost virginity and virtue.

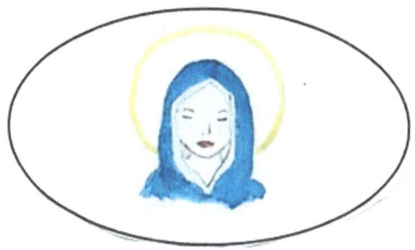

47. Virgin Mary

- **Blue / white / pink / red dress or robe**
- **Tree of life**: wisdom, protection, strength, and beauty.
- **Enclosed Garden**: the Ever-Virgin Mary
- Spotless **mirror**: Holy Virgin's immaculate conception and purity
- **Crown**: queen of heaven
- **Unicorn**: lets himself be tamed only by a Virgin
- **Rosemary; rose**: rose without thorns (i.e. sinless).
- **Iris & Lilies**: sign of Mary's purity
- Open **book**: wisdom
- **Olive**: peace and concord
- **Palm**: martyrdom

In many religions mother figures are worshipped, and the Virgin Mary is one of the most depicted subject matters in Western Art.

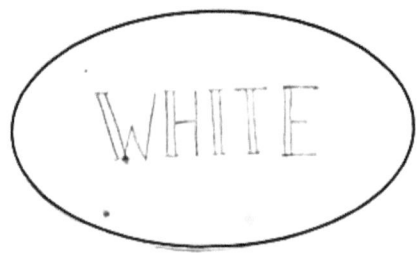

48. White (the colour)

- Innocence; Birth; Youth
- Betrothal and Marriage; (sexual) purity
- The Virgin Mary; The Immaculate Conception
- Peace; sacrifice
- Light

White is the colour which is produced by combining all the colours of the colour spectrum. (Don't try this at home, by mixing all your paints, because you'll just end up with an ugly brown!)

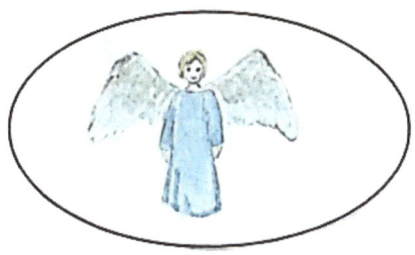

49. Winged figure

- Mythology:
  - **Victoria** (Roman) / **Nike** (Greek): mythological goddess who brings the message of victory
  - **Hermes** (Roman) /**Mercury** (Greek): guide of the gods, his wings are attached to his hat and feet, and carries a staff with two snakes curling around it.
  - **Cupid or Putto** (Roman) / **Eros** (Greek): son of Venus/ Aphrodite, goddess of love; other attributes: bees, blindfold (love is blind), weapons (power of love), bow and arrow (his golden arrows made people fall in love, his lead arrows made people hate each other)
- Christianity:
  - **Angel / cherub**: messenger of God

- o   **Archangels** Gabriel, Michael and Raphael
- Allegorical figures:
  - o   **Fame**
  - o   **Peace**
  - o   **Fortune; opportunity**
  - o   **Father Time**
  - o   **Melancholy; night**

Figures are often marked as divine by their wings. Human beings have always been mesmerised by the idea of flying under their own power. Many people dream of flying, and for a long time it was seen as only possible for those with special powers (deities etc). Flying takes place in the space between the earth and the heavens, which makes winged figures the perfect symbols for crossing between the two.

50. *Yellow: See 30. Orange*

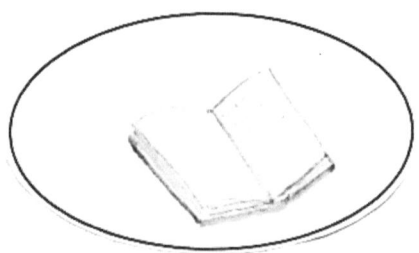

Bibliography

Bérard, C., A City of Images: Iconography and Society in Ancient Greece (Princeton, 1989).

Bell, Robert E, Dictionary of classical mythology symbols, attributes, and associations (Santa Barbara, CA, 1982)

An Illustrated Encyclopaedia of Traditional Symbols, J.C. Cooper, (Thames & Hudson, 1978)

Colour and Meaning. Art, Science and Symbolism, by John Gage (Thames & Hudson, 1999)

The Theology of Arithmetic: On the Mystical, Mathematical and Cosmological Symbolism of the First Ten Numbers, by Iamblichus; Robin Waterfield, Keith Critchlow, Translated by Robin Waterfield (Phanes Press, 1988)

1000 Symbols: What Shapes Mean in Art and Myth, by Rowena Shepherd and Rupert Shepherd (Thames & Hudson, 2002)

Cosmatesque Ornament: Flat Polychrome Geometric Patterns in Architecture, by Paloma Pajares-Ayuela (Thames & Hudson, 2002)

Piero della Fancesca in America, Frick Collection New York (New York, 2013)

The Embarrassment of Riches, an interpretation of Dutch Culture in the Golden Age, Simon Schama, Fontana Press (1991)

Lucie-Smith, Edward. Symbolist Art. London: Thames & Hudson, 2001.

Mathieu, Pierre-Louis. The Symbolist Generation, 1870–1910. New York: Skira, 1990.

Michelle Facos. Symbolist Art in Context. University of California Press, 17 April 2009

Richard Thomson and Rodolphe Rapetti. Van Gogh to Kandinsky: Symbolist Landscape in Europe 1880-1910. Thames & Hudson, 14 May 2012

www.ingramcontent.com/pod product-compliance
Lightning Source LLC
Chambersburg PA
CBHW040905180526
45159CB00010BA/2941